What Is Evangelism?

Basics of the Faith

Am I Called?
How Do We Glorify God?
How Our Children Come to Faith
Is Jesus in the Old Testament?
What Are Election and Predestination?
What Are Spiritual Gifts?
What Happens after Death?
What Is a Reformed Church?
What Is a True Calvinist?
What Is Biblical Preaching?
What Is Church Government?
What Is Discipleship?
What Is Evangelism?
What Is Faith?
What Is Grace?
What Is Hell?
What Is Justification by Faith Alone?
What Is Man?
What Is Mercy Ministry?
What Is Perseverance of the Saints?
What Is Providence?
What Is Regeneration?
What Is Spiritual Warfare?
What Is the Atonement?
What Is the Bible?
What Is the Christian Worldview?
What Is the Doctrine of Adoption?
What Is the Incarnation?
What Is the Lord's Supper?
What Is the Trinity?
What Is True Conversion?
What Is Vocation?
What Is Worship Music?
Why Believe in God?
Why Do We Baptize Infants?
Why Do We Have Creeds?
Why Do We Pray?
Why God Gave Us a Book

Sean Michael Lucas, Series Editor

What Is Evangelism?

George W. Robertson

P&R
PUBLISHING
P.O. BOX 817 • PHILLIPSBURG • NEW JERSEY 08865-0817

ISBN: 978-1-59638-766-9 (pbk)
ISBN: 978-1-59638-767-6 (ePub)
ISBN: 978-1-59638-768-3 (Mobi)

Page design by Tobias Design

Printed in the United States of America

Library of Congress Cataloging-in-Publication Data

Robertson, George W. (George William), 1966-
What is evangelism? / George W. Robertson.
pages cm. -- (Basics of the faith)
Includes bibliographical references.
ISBN 978-1-59638-766-9 (pbk.)
1. Evangelistic work. I. Title.
BV3790.R564 2013
269'.2--dc23

2013030444

PROCLAMATION, PERSUASION, PRAYER

What is evangelism? How could a term so basic to the Christian faith be the subject of such divergent opinions? Opinions range between two extremes: those who think that evangelism is any church activity and those who consider someone evangelized only when he or she becomes a disciple of Jesus Christ and a responsible member of a local church.[1] Rather than defining evangelism, the Bible describes it. Our English word is a transliteration of the Greek word *euangelizo*, which means "to proclaim good news." And that is what is being described when the word is used in Scripture—someone's declaring the good news of salvation in Jesus Christ (Luke 9:6; 20:1; Acts 8:25, 40; 16:10; Rom. 1:9, 15; 15:20; 1 Cor. 1:17; 9:14, 16, 18; 2 Cor. 11:7; Gal. 1:11; 2:2, 7; 4:13; 1 Thess. 2:9; 1 Peter 1:12; 4:6). While those occurrences are typically translated "preach the gospel," there are only a few occasions when the gospel is said explicitly to be "preached" (*kerux*) (Matt. 24:14; 26:13; Mark 13:10; 14:9). Ordinarily, the action of one person or a group taking the gospel to unbelievers is just described as "good-news telling." The most basic thing then that can be said about evangelism is that it is any manner of *proclaiming* the good news of Jesus Christ.

Though they did not know all the details of Jesus' incarnation and sacrifice, Old Testament believers were not bereft of the good news. The message of redemption proclaimed to the people of God from the time of Abraham to Moses is also called "the gospel" (Gal. 3:8; Heb. 4:2, 6). Additionally, Paul desired to "preach the gospel" to the "saints" in Rome (1:7, 15). So the argument could be made that the whole Bible is the gospel and to preach any of it therefore is to preach good news. However, the focus of this booklet is on proclaiming the salvific work of Jesus Christ in such a manner that those who have never done so will receive him by faith and prove their regeneration with discipleship.[2]

Jesus' parables and the example of the apostles lead us to conclude that the good news is so great that it must be proclaimed with a desire to *persuade* (Luke 14:23; Acts 18:4; 2 Cor. 5:11). The Bible never hints that the herald is the converter. Persuasion or conversion is possible only when the Spirit removes a "heart of stone" and replaces it with a "heart of flesh" (Ezek. 36:26) and "opens" it to receive the free offer of grace (Acts 16:40). That means that the believer's responsibility is not just to proclaim the gospel but also to *pray* for its effectiveness as the Holy Spirit applies it to the heart. Interestingly, the Bible never commands or even describes believers praying for people to be converted; rather they pray for "more laborers" (Matt. 9:37), "open doors" (Col. 4:3), and "boldness" (Acts 4:29). The implication seems to be that praying for someone's heart to change would give the impression that somehow the power to convert lies within the person. Praying for multiplication of witnesses, opportunities to speak, and courage to persist against opposition emphasizes that all the gospel's power comes from God. It comes from the Holy Spirit who empowers its ambassadors (Acts 1:8), who in turn through the "foolishness" of proclamation (1 Cor. 1:21) have the privilege of unleashing a message that conquers unbelief.

One final preliminary remark is important. Since evangelism is the message of Jesus Christ who incarnated all God's promises, the gospel contains good news for every human need. It is like an expensive diamond containing so many facets by means of the master cutter's hand that it sparkles with light no matter how it is turned. A couple of scholars put the point this way: "[Evangelism] is the communication of the whole gospel in simple form, along with a concern to address intellectual hindrances to faith or those deriving from experience."[3]

In 1974 the first Lausanne Congress for world evangelization immediately felt the need to express the enterprise of evangelism in holistic terms. Convener René Padilla said the Lausanne Covenant showed that "biblical evangelism is inseparable from social responsibility, Christian discipleship, and church renewal."[4] In an era in which the evangelical church seeks to incarnate the gospel in practical service while preserving an emphasis on conversion, the clear delineation of these two concerns in paragraph five of the covenant is worth quoting: "When people receive Christ they are born again into his kingdom and must seek not only to exhibit but also to spread its righteousness in the midst of an unrighteous world. The salvation we claim should be transforming us in the totality of our personal and social responsibilities. Faith without works is dead."[5]

Notwithstanding this effort to define evangelism, I must say, as a pastor, that when people ask me what evangelism is, they are only slightly helped by the preacher's three Ps: proclamation, persuasion, and prayer. Usually, what they are really asking is, "What does evangelism look like in my life?" Here they need five points rather than three. I claim no originality for these five points. Those who take the Scriptures seriously have long observed these five ways in which the gospel is communicated in such a manner that someone converts to

Christianity. However, I want to distance myself a bit from those who in recent years have given the impression that these are five different *options* for doing evangelism. Some have even linked these various approaches to individual personality types, leaving the impression that effective evangelism begins with understanding yourself and then proclaiming the gospel in a way that is comfortable. I share the pastoral desire of these good thinkers to liberate those who live in the defeated idea that they cannot be evangelists because they cannot give their faith away just like someone else they admire. However, it would be less than Christlike to begin with yourself in the evangelistic task. Jesus humbled himself as a servant because we were in need (Phil. 2:1–11). Likewise, we must first ask what someone without Christ needs: What communicates to him? What physical needs does she have? What relational challenges does he face? What word does the gospel speak into her distress? Then we must find a way to apply the good news to that need. This is the attitude of a servant-evangelist like Christ. While an individual may identify with some of these categories or styles or methodologies more readily than others, all must be studied out of love for the lost and gratitude for the grace of Christ.

TESTIMONIAL

That said, the most logical starting point is with what every Christian has—a testimony of grace. Testimonial evangelism is telling others what Christ has done for you. While there may be some who are especially gifted at giving their testimony, everyone who has been saved has a story to tell. Psalm 126 describes testimonial evangelism as well as any text of Scripture. In it the psalmist calls each believer to recall God's grace from the past and take confidence in the same for the future. Specifically, he exhorts believers to get in touch with the joy of it. While some Christians are more naturally joyful than others, each must constantly rediscover the joy of salvation so that he or she can better testify to it. At the very center of the psalm is this testimony: "We are filled with joy" (v. 3). The speakers are joyful because they have been delivered from the agony of their Babylonian exile and are finally living in the restoration they previously could only have dreamed of.

The first step to testimonial evangelism then is taking time to meditate on one's redemption (vv. 1–3). When the captives left their bonds, they were so joyful that they were like "men who dreamed" (v. 1). They had never expected to be released. They had been in exile for seventy years, so they had lost hope. The experience had been as horrific as any holocaust history ever written. They had been violated, reduced to cannibalism and beastly behavior, and forced to walk six hundred miles under their captors' jeers.[6] So when they were released and returned to their homeland, they were delirious with joy. However, the Israelites' return to Jerusalem was not just one of many happy events in the Bible; it was a redemptive-historical event designed by God to prepare God's people for the infinitely greater joy that would come through the Messiah. Christians should be equally delirious with joy. Hebrews 12:22–24 clearly identifies our coming home to Christ as the antetype of Mt. Zion—to come home to a relationship with the Father through Christ is to experience real and cosmic joy.

But that joy must be transformed into a spoken testimony. Psalm 126 illustrates that it need not be profound. It can be as simple as that of the pilgrims: "The LORD has done great things for us" (v. 3). It is a good idea to prepare a brief but brilliant personal testimony that one can deliver with confidence at a moment's notice. One should have a version one can share within three minutes, but that is capable of expansion into three hours. Here is a simple three-point outline: "What my life was like before Christ. How Christ transformed my life through the gospel. And finally, the difference Christ has made in my life since he saved me."

John Wesley mobilized his Methodists by urging them to tell their story whether or not they were in the mood:

> We have known many instances of this; persons cold and dull, and scarce known how to believe their own words, have asserted, as they could, the truths of the gospel, and enforced them upon others, and at that very time God has caused light and love to spring up in their own hearts. Therefore, however you feel it in your own breast, speak as well as you can for God. Many times you will see some fruit upon others.[7]

The Methodists, like generations of Christians before them, proved that if a testimony shared perfunctorily can be used to win a lost soul, one shared joyfully will be especially contagious. Of course only the elect are drawn to salvation, but even the elect are attracted more often by a joyful testimony than by a dour one. In Psalm 126, the Israelites are speaking to one another. Christians have a responsibility not only to tell unbelievers that the Lord has done great things for them, but also, like these pilgrims, to encourage one another with the same gospel. Not only so, but when the Gentiles overhear their joy, they conclude that the Lord had done great things for his people (cf. Isa. 52:10). Sharing a testimony is not self-aggrandizing, but rather points others to how great God is.

To relate a testimony in a meaningful way means that one must first listen carefully to the addressee. The testifier's goal must be to relate his or her life to that person's life, not just convey a message. Though their backgrounds may be very different, both are broken human beings living in broken world, created by the same God. A testimony that connects is one that relates how Christ met broken conditions that are universally shared: guilt, loneliness, confusion, anxiety, anger, hate, pride, apathy, estrangement, and so on. The only difference among human beings then is whether one is being saved by grace or not.

The most remarkable portion of this psalm is in verses 4–6, which explain the grief that the Israelites felt as the devastation of Jerusalem sank into their hearts. They went about their work of rebuilding, but with tears and remorse (Hag. 2:3–9, 17–19). This is remarkable because the psalmist says that even during this time they were "filled with joy" (Ps. 126:3). It is not coincidental that God's people in the Old Testament knew joy mingled with weeping as they rebuilt Mount Zion on earth; it was an experience designed by God to teach his people in all ages that, as difficult as it is to live for Christ the King on earth, we have a deeper joy in knowing that his is a kingdom that cannot fail. Christians must be defiantly joyful people because God's Spirit dwells in them, even when they see no hope for their earthly situation. The image is of a new farmer sowing his seeds in the Negev in the southern part of Israel, praying all the while that God would cause this desert to flow with streams of water (cf. Jer. 31:9). Lo and behold, the winter comes and the wadis, which have been dry for the last eleven months, fill up and become raging torrents. The evangelist must pray that God would use his or her feeble efforts at sharing the gospel and working for him in this culture to do the same.

At the same time, no true Christian can remain passive. The intensity of the Hebrew makes that especially clear in this psalm. The verbs are doubled, so verse 6 could be translated, "He who surely goes forth weeping will surely come home with shouts of joy." Note the intensity of motive: the people are going about their work so faithfully because they passionately care for their city and what it represents for the glory of God. Likewise, the one who will be an effective soul winner is one who cares deeply for lost souls and sheds tears for them. To be effective in prayer for and in witnessing to the lost, Christians must be emotionally moved by their condition. When the Bible says a real person without Christ will never know true joy in this world and will live forever in a place where the fire is never quenched and the worm of death never dies, a Christian will be moved to take whatever risks necessary to share the good news.

There is no better illustration of the point of this passage than the story in John 9 of the man born blind. Jesus' disciples asked why this man was blind, thinking that the reason had to be that either he had sinned or his parents had sinned. Jesus said it was neither. He had been born blind so that the glory of God would be displayed in his life. Then Jesus applied mud made with his own saliva to the man's eyes and told him to wash in the Pool of Siloam. After he washed, he could see. The religious leaders then pounded him with theological questions. After trying vainly to answer, he simply said, "One thing I do know. I was blind but now I see!" (v. 25). That simple testimony made a profound impact. Yes, it cost him: he was kicked out of the synagogue. But his testimony is recorded forever in Scripture and has been the instrument of leading thousands to Christ over two thousand years. Surely this man could have thought his life was useless and could accomplish nothing, but Christ continues to use his simple testimony to display the works of God. You do not have to be an intellectual, a theologian, beautiful, strong, or influential. If you have a testimony that Christ has saved you, you know enough to share a testimony that God can use mightily.

INVITATIONAL

However, a testimony is not an end in itself—explicitly or implicitly it is an invitation to come to the Savior. Jesus commands invitational evangelism in Luke 14:15–24, the parable of the great banquet. Another banquet preceded this one in verses 1–14. Hosted at a prominent Pharisee's house, Jesus used a parable intentionally to offend every guest who was resting in his self-righteousness. This parable was provoked by the exclamation in verse 15, "Blessed is the man who will eat at the feast in the kingdom of God." These self-serving religious leaders were fond of thinking about the banquet that would be spread for them by a God in heaven who owed it to them—a banquet at which there would be only Jews and no Gentile "dogs." Jesus' parable would offend, shock, and surprise by its description of the expanse of God's gracious invitation.

A lavish feast is pictured in these early verses. It is to be a "great banquet" with "many guests" (v. 16), hosted by an obviously wealthy man with servants at his beck and call. Jesus is thinking of the wedding supper of the Lamb described in Revelation 19. There is nothing stingy or conservative implied here. It was the custom of Jesus' day to give two invitations. The first one would be a written announcement, describing the date and place. If the guest responded positively to the first invitation, then a servant would deliver a second one on the night of the event. The Midrash on Lamentations said of the men of Jerusalem, "None of them would attend a banquet unless he was invited twice."[8] To accept the first and refuse the second would be unconscionable. But that is precisely what these three guests did, and each with very lame excuses.

But Jesus was really presenting categories of excuses for not coming to God's rich spread of grace. The first two excuses represent possessions, and the last represents relationships.

Possessions and relationships keep many a person from responding to the generous invitation of the gospel. Possessions and relationships keep many a person from responding to a simple invitation to come to church. Such refusals must not discourage, because no matter how much enjoyment anyone has in his or her possessions or relationships, there is infinitely more to be discovered in a life with Christ. Jesus spreads a table laden with graces such as a clean conscience, peace that passes understanding, joy unspeakable, abundant life, freedom from worry, release from bondage to self, fearlessness of death, forgiveness of sin, a relationship with a heavenly Father, true love, daily guidance, eternal wisdom, an abundance of loving family members, and purpose. It is to this generous feast that a Christian is privileged to invite anyone.

Neither should discretion be a concern; Jesus said the doors of his banquet hall are opened to all the world's untouchables. Jesus probably intended to communicate two things by this list. First, Jesus made it clear that he was opening the doors of God's grace to the Gentiles. That was a shocking and offensive message to these Jewish religious leaders. The Jews were fond of painting mental images of what this great banquet would be like when the Messiah would invade their world and set up his kingdom. They imagined that the great sea monster, Leviathan, would be one of the main dishes.[9] They knew they would be there, Leviathan might or might not be there, but for sure the Gentiles would not be there. But Jesus said otherwise, and the book of Acts would prove him right (13:46; 18:6; 28:23–28). And there was another group that Jesus was pointing to—the disenfranchised. They were the poor, the crippled, the blind, and the lame, who since Moses' day had been excluded even from temple worship (Lev. 21:17–23). These he promised would hear the gospel from his missionaries and find a seat at the great wedding supper of the Lamb.

Here are some practical suggestions for inviting people to church. First, relax by recognizing that God is sovereign over all situations and that he is the one who converts. As a new Christian, I was hypersensitive to every detail when I brought unbelievers to my home church. I scrutinized everything mercilessly, wanting it to be perfect for my friends. I criticized the sermon because it was not evangelistic enough, or my fellow members because they were not friendly enough, or the music because it was not attractive enough. Finally I realized that I was trying to control everything rather than living as though God alone saves. Relax and rest on God's sovereignty.

Second, invite children especially. The statistics for child conversion are remarkable. The conversion rate for children between ages five and thirteen is 32 percent. Between fourteen and eighteen it drops precipitously to 4 percent. For eighteen-year-olds and up it rises slightly to 6 percent.[10] Encourage children to invite unsaved friends to church and invite the kids of unsaved neighbors to church. Finally, invite people to anything. Especially invite them to any service or ministry where the Word of God is being expounded. Thom Rainer studied 576 of the most effective evangelistic churches in the country and discovered what he called "Ten Surprises." The number one surprise to him was that event evangelism—that is, things such as concerts and carnivals—does not work. Few people make professions of faith as a result of these, and next to none of those continue on in discipleship. Another surprise is that a church may do lots of evangelistic training and still be ineffective in reaching the lost. Another was that most effective evangelistic churches do not offer seeker services. The number one method for reaching the lost was members telling others about Christ. The second most effective was inviting the lost to a service where the Word was preached. His conclusion was that effective evangelistic churches are those that focus on just a few things: namely biblical preaching, prayer, intentional witnessing, missions, and Sunday school.[11] Acknowledge how powerful the Word is in the Spirit's hands. The whole Bible is gospel, and the Spirit can take the diamond of the Word of God and turn it so that it beams its light into the heart in precisely the right way. Spurgeon said that he was often amazed at which doctrines the Spirit would use to convert. For one it was the resurrection, for another election, and yet others the law.[12] The point is that the Spirit can use any portion of the Bible to convert, not just the ones on repentance and faith. Dare to invite and let the Spirit work.

Finally, notice the urgency of the invitation (Luke 14:23–24). The master commands his servant to "make them come in." The King James Version said, "compel them to come in." Much harm has been done historically by the misinterpretation of that verse to justify all violent means for converting "infidels." But clearly Jesus intended his followers to urgently beg people to come to Christ. On the one hand, his witnesses must persuade unbelievers that grace is adequate for them regardless of their unworthiness. And on the other hand, Christians must compel their neighbors to come to Christ for shelter in view of the coming judgment.

Charles Spurgeon told an arresting story about two athletes in his church who made it their habit to invite people to attend church with them. On one occasion they stopped and gave a shopkeeper a tract. The merchant said, "What is the use of this tract? I shall be in hell in an hour!" After the two runners conferred, they decided he was either insane or determined to commit suicide. Fearing the latter, one said, "Then we will be after him." They followed the man and asked him what he meant, and he told them it was none of their business. So one of the athletes said, "But it is my business, for, if I heard aright, you said that you would be in hell in an hour." The man confirmed that they had heard correctly, and that since the world was worse than hell, he planned to be out of it in an hour. They determined from his looks that he needed a good meal. That perked him up a bit to the point that he agreed to go to church with them. Afterward they had him back to their humble home and fed him a hearty lunch, and he returned to evening services with them. That evening he was converted. Soon he explained that he had run away from his wife and had been living away from home for months. They found his home, bought him a train ticket, and sent him back to his wife in the north of England. Later she wrote them and relayed that she too was a Christian and had given up all hope for her husband when he left. But now she knew God loved him more and knew no more indescribable joy than to celebrate the Lord's Supper with her newfound Christian husband.[13] With both judgment and grace clearly in his or her view, a Christian must not delay inviting friends to come and hear about Christ.

INTENTIONAL

Concern for the eternal state of souls means evangelism cannot be restricted to those occasions when an opportunity clearly presents itself. To be an evangelist is to be intentional about sharing the gospel with unbelievers. In 1 Corinthians 9, Paul commanded believers to become the slave of every other human being for the sake of the gospel, that some might be won. Paul exemplified his exhortation by yielding his rights to everyone else in order to advance the gospel. For one to become this kind of slave requires conscious preparation to limit one's freedoms, draw close to those who have no limits, and be consumed by the call of grace.

One must be willing to place limits on his or her rights to win some for Christ (v. 20). Remember, Paul ministered among two radically different groups of people—devoutly religious Jews and absolutely irreligious Gentiles. For one, the precise practice of the 613 laws of the Old Testament plus numerous additional codes was essential to salvation. For the other, each person's conduct was determined and limited only by civic penalty. In between these, Paul steered a carefully balanced course. In matters of indifference, Paul yielded readily. However, in matters of biblical principle, Paul never compromised. That is how he could say in one breath that he was free from the law (vv. 19–20) and in the next that he was under the law of Christ (v. 21). He meant that because he was free from the enslaving idea that the law saves, he was liberated to respond gratefully to Christ's grace by keeping the Ten Commandments and their implications.

Therefore, to reach the Jews who were under the sad delusion that they had to keep God's law meticulously *in order* to be saved, he willingly submitted to some of their requirements. For instance, in order to reach Jews in Jerusalem, he had his four companions shave their heads and engage in purification rites (Acts 21:18–27). Those were indifferent matters. Paul was perfectly willing to yield to such rules as long as his doing so did not send the message that he was doing so as a means of earning salvation. In fact, when having Titus circumcised could have given that impression, he absolutely refused (Gal. 2:3). It is probable that limiting one's freedom is the hardest exercise of slavery. It is much harder than associating with those who are free from any restrictions because we seldom look for ways to live less freely.

Additionally, the apostle explained that there are times when a Christian must put himself or herself in uncomfortable situations in order to win those "not having the law" (1 Cor. 9:21). Of course he is referring now to Gentiles who did not even know about the Jewish laws. These are the ones with whom Paul would have eaten nonkosher food or meat offered first to idols, something very uncomfortable for a strict Jew. But he knew that he had been set free from extrabiblical strictures, and despite his cultural discomfort he would engage in such practices not to flaunt his freedom but to win the lost.

Most contemporary Christians are surrounded by those who have few conscientious scruples and little religious training. What will becoming a servant to them for the gospel's sake look like? It may mean sitting in the break room with people who tell off-color jokes and use the Lord's name in vain. It may mean going to a concert of an artist you do not appreciate, because an unbeliever has invited you. It may mean attending a party where no one shares the same values as you and the talk is all of getting ahead. It may mean listening to someone's syncretistic spiritual ideas. The Christlike evangelist must go where unbelievers are and expect to come out smelling like the sewer that engulfs them. He or she must not insist on conversing only after the unbeliever cleans up his mouth or changes her ways or comes to church or sits well behaved in the living room.

Such evangelism can be dangerous. Of course Christ's ambassador must not engage in the same sinful activities and behaviors as unbelievers. Obviously if a certain context is overwhelmingly tempting, then a Christian must not go there. He or she can pray for another messenger. An alcoholic must not go to bars to witness, and no Christian should watch sexually tempting movies or listen to music that entices her to sin. If you have questions about the parameters of such endeavors, talk to a trusted spiritual counselor. No matter the safeguards, daring to step into the unbeliever's world is to risk criticism from other Christians. There are Christians who believe that their contrived rules are more important than winning souls and that the essence of the Christian life is *not doing* certain things. Some Christians are even threatened by evangelists because it causes them guilt to see others evangelizing when they are not. The obedient Christian must be gentle and patient with such gainsayers (Rom. 14:1; 1 Cor. 8:13). But there may come a time when their hypocrisy must be confronted to preserve the reputation of the gospel. Remember, Paul rebuked Peter for turning his back on the Gentiles when his Jewish friends began to criticize him (Gal. 2:11–21). Evangelism can be dangerous both inside and outside the walls of the church.

Scholars are uncertain about whom Paul had in mind when he referred to the "weak" (1 Cor. 9:22). It could be another reference to the Gentiles who were unconverted or even newly converted. He could be referring to the weak of conscience, such as Jewish Christians who could not yet shake their ceremonial restrictions. These are the ones, he says in Romans 14 and 1 Corinthians 8, whom more mature Christians must be careful not to offend unnecessarily. So around these he would not eat food offered to idols or consume a nonkosher meal. Some think that Paul is referring to the economically weak since he has just been discussing the fact that he is "free" from all men as a tentmaker (1 Cor. 9:19). Therefore, he would be saying that even though he is well educated, well bred, and well-to-do, he became as one poor to reach the poor. It is not necessary to determine whether the weak are Jews or Gentiles, Christians or non-Christians, rich or poor. The simple point is that they are weak and need to be brought closer to Christ, and in order to do that he became like them, however uncomfortable it was.

Like Paul, the Christian must be consumed with furthering the gospel. Paul became as one under the law and fraternized with those not under the law in order to share the gospel with them. He limited his freedom around weak Christians so that they would not shut him down before he had opportunity to share with them the freedom the gospel brings. He labored to bring Euodia and Syntyche together in harmony at the church of Philippi so that the gospel would not be hindered (Phil. 4:2–3). He agonized over the church at Corinth that was not disciplining an errant member, because outsiders were beginning to scorn the gospel (1 Cor. 5:1). Likewise, every Christian's life exists for the sake of the gospel. We order our lives in a godly way before our children so that they will not only embrace the gospel but also share it with their friends. We do our work excellently so that no scorn is brought upon the gospel. We look for open doors in conversations to speak a word for the gospel. Every Christian should wake up and ask, "What am I going to do for the sake of the gospel today?" And every evening when he retires, he should ask, "What did I do for the gospel today and how did I hinder it?" And when he confesses to Christ where he's hindered the message, then he must tell Christ again that he loves him and desires to see the same good news that he received spread to others.

Notice finally that Paul is zealous to see the gospel spread through his life that he might "share in its blessings" (1 Cor. 9:23). He obviously did not mean that by spreading the Word he merited a spiritual reward. Rather, he knew that living for the gospel results in even more benefits from the gospel. Perhaps the greatest blessing to Paul was seeing others transformed by the same power that transformed him. He loved these Corinthians before they were saved, and he loved them all the more afterward. He called them his letters written on his heart by the Spirit (2 Cor. 3:2) and pleaded with them through tears when they erred (2 Cor. 2:4). That is the blessing of the gospel—the indescribable love that knits together the bearer of the good news and the one who is transformed by it. Intentional evangelism is essentially listening and loving.

COMPASSIONATE

Compassionate and practical acts of service open doors for the gospel. This is what Jesus envisioned in the Sermon on the Mount (Matt. 5:13–16). These words follow on the heels of what Jesus teaches to be the norms of the Christian life, otherwise known as the Beatitudes. In other words, a true Christian's life will be characterized by humility, mourning over sin, meekness, hunger and thirst for righteousness, purity of heart, and peacemaking. These are the norms because they are created in the Christian by the Holy Spirit as implied by the word *blessed*. However, in this portion of his sermon, Jesus said that such a life cannot be hidden or lived in isolation. It will inevitably become public. And that life, Jesus assured his hearers, will lead others to either conversion or opposition and maybe even persecution (cf. vv. 43–44). In other words, the Lord of the harvest ensures that his gospel will go forth through lives yielded to the Holy Spirit.

One of the great heroes of the history of missions is Robert Lamb, a New Zealander who became a missionary doctor to the swagmen of Australia. He did not have the health to travel and preach, so he landed on another plan. Discovering a log at the bend of a road, he sat there and greeted the poor workmen who passed by with heavy burdens on their shoulders. Every morning he would take his seat on the log and give them some refreshment and then turn the conversation to the gospel. Before he said good-bye to a new friend, he would give him a New Testament and read to him Jesus' invitation, "Come to Me, all who are weary and heavy-laden" (Matt. 11:28 RSV). This man led many to Christ by ministering mercy. Their hearts were first opened by a practical demonstration of love, and then the gospel could enter more effectively. His good works, in other words, led others to glorify the same God. That is the phenomenon that Jesus described in his sermon.

Those whose lives are yielded to the Holy Spirit will be "salt" in the earth. It is difficult to know all that Jesus had in mind when he said that his disciples' lives would be salty, but reflecting on what salt does brings some insight. We know at least this much: salt preserves and seasons. The comparison is encouraging because, though cheap, salt accomplishes great things. For example, just as salt preserves, Christians have proven throughout church history to be preserving influences in their culture, even if they are a minority. Small bands of Christians have made a great difference in saving unwanted children, abolishing slavery, reforming education, obtaining justice for the poor, protecting workers' rights, stewarding the environment, and caring for animals. As salt, Christians can preserve an organization or community from being destroyed by its ungodliness.

Jesus could have had a couple of Old Testament images of salt in his mind as he spoke these words. For instance, he could have been thinking about Ezekiel 16:4 and the ancient hygienic practice of rubbing a newborn with salt to cleanse her, thus calling his followers to live as preservative influences in the world as early as possible. Covenant parents must challenge their children and young Christians to start living out the norms of the Christian life as soon as possible. Perhaps he also had the image of Judges 9:45 in his mind. There Abimelech the judge scattered salt over Shechem after defeating it. Since salt makes soil infertile, Abimelech's action was a kind of prayer that another evil city would not rise up from Shechem's soil. That is what Christians do when they publicly live righteous lives: they arrest sin.[14] Christians may be few and powerless, but by the Spirit they can change whole organizations.

There is also a warning here. Jesus alerted his disciples that if they did not live preservatively, they would become useless for the kingdom. Some opine that Jesus implied that Christians cannot help but witness because it is part of their nature, just like salt can never not be salt. However, salt can become corrupted to the point that it becomes useless. For instance, it can get wet or mixed with sand. Even so, Christians can become diluted by the world. They can choose to live more by the spirit of the world than the Spirit of the Beatitudes. And if so, they could become as useless to the kingdom as Lot was to Sodom. Out of love for the Savior an evangelist must continually plead that the Spirit would make him or her effective for Christ and his kingdom.

Salt not only preserves, it seasons. Salt adds flavor and zest. Whether a natural extrovert or not, a Christian should have the ability to add joy to any occasion even as Jesus did. His or her mere presence should bring blessing rather than misery. In this regard, Jesus could have had in his mind another image of salt from the Old Testament. In Leviticus 2:13, the Lord commanded worshipers to add salt to the offerings. Some commentators explain that salt was a symbol of faithfulness; that is, the salt symbolized the person's heart being given along with the sacrifice. That is to say, it visibly confessed, "I am not just giving my sacrifice as bare duty; I am giving my heart with it." Such sacrifices of the heart bless God, and that attitude blesses others.

Interestingly, in the New Testament the one activity of a Christian that is specifically said must be like salt is speech. For instance, Paul insisted that our speech must be "seasoned with salt" (Col. 4:6). It is in the parallel verse in Ephesians 4:29 that we find what that means—to speak only that which is helpful in building others up. Building others up for Christ is among the greatest services that can be rendered for the sake of the gospel.

Jesus then turned to another image to describe the effect of a Christian's good works in the world by calling Christians "the light of the world" (Matt. 5:14). By definition a Christian is to be a light. Further, as a member of the kingdom of God he or she is part of a city whose light cannot be hidden. He was assuring his hearers that the Holy Spirit always maintains a witness in the world through a faithful remnant of the church. Though a large segment of the church may be hiding her witness for the time being, somewhere the Holy Spirit maintains some embers. While individual Christians may blend in with the rest of the world, God maintains a corporate witness somewhere. Therefore, while Jesus does not say that it is impossible for a Christian to hide his light, he does say that it is illogical and unnatural (v. 15). It makes no sense to hide a light when people need a light. Likewise, a Christian must lead a publicly obedient life for the Savior because the world desperately needs it. To compromise or to pretend that one is not a Christian is ultimately a hateful thing. It is like standing on the edge of a precipice shrouded in darkness while people are falling over it to their deaths, and refusing to turn on your flashlight because you do not want people to know you are any different.

Guidance into the life of salvation is a major implication of this image. A lighted city on a hill is a welcome sight to a lost traveler. When one gets into the countryside away from all the city's bright lamps, one can more easily imagine how important a light on a hill would be to a pilgrim on an uncharted journey. Paul says evangelists must be guides and that such guidance comes from the Holy Spirit's leadership. When Christians let their light shine, they attract others to Christ and a relationship with God the Father. Ultimately, Jesus commands living out the norms of the Christian life so that people will see the better way and be attracted to such a benevolent King. Light is attractive. People like well-lit places unless they are trying to hide their actions. Likewise, lives lived compassionately are attractive, especially to the downtrodden. The evangelist must pray for the Spirit's enabling power—power to preserve, power to shine, power to attract, power to call to conversion.

INTELLECTUAL

Paul's encounter with Athenian philosophers in Acts 17:16–34 exemplifies the intellectual challenges of apologetics, which include answering the unbeliever's questions, silencing false accusations against the gospel, and leading seekers to personal trust in Christ. However, this is not a task restricted to philosophers; God's ordinary people are capable of demonstrating the relevance of the gospel. For example, it was ordinary people who answered the questions of one of the brightest thinkers in the public square, Glenn Loury. In an epilogue to his book on combating racism in this generation, Loury related his personal conversion to Jesus Christ:

> What happened for me was that some people came forward to offer words about the Gospel. . . . People proclaimed to me the availability of salvation and the fact that there was a way out. People asked me to consider the words of Jesus . . . *I have come to save that which is lost. . . . I am the way, the truth and the life; no one comes to the Father but through me. . . . When the Son sets you free, you shall be free indeed. . . .* Nothing was quite the same again after that.[15]

By virtue of the Spirit who works by and with the Scriptures, every Christian has within his or her worldview the answers to human need. As overwhelming as those needs may be—political, social, financial, educational, medical, legal—Christians must not shrink back. The gospel has always provided the foundation from which all these problems can be addressed temporally and eternally.

The first key to presenting the faith in an intellectually credible way is to make a studied effort to understand the context of the person one intends to reach. Paul and Luke understood the Athenian mindset. Although twenty-seven years of war with Sparta had toppled Athens from its place of political domination, it nevertheless remained an intellectual capital. Paul knew the power that such a place of learning held, so he entered the city ready to take on its two main philosophies: Epicureanism and Stoicism. The Epicureans lived only for the present, and the Stoics were fatalists.

The dominant present-day worldviews are similar. Like Stoicism, postmodernism is a fatalistic, morbid, and hopeless perspective. While promising freedom from previous imperialistic philosophies, it ultimately enslaves one to fear because nothing is predictable or reliable. And like the Epicurean mindset, personal enjoyment is the preferred contemporary idol. It is what drives many to avoid responsibility, relationships, group activities, generosity, and heroism, because these things require sacrifice. Millions are willing to expend large portions of energy and great sums of money to avoid pain and obtain pleasure. How does the evangelist give an answer for the hope within him to someone who is either entirely distraught or highly comfortable? Paul's sermon in verses 22–31 before the influential colloquy of philosophers in Athens is an exemplary methodology for how we can apply the gospel to these kinds of intellectual challenges to the faith.

His first strategy was to find a point of contact between biblical truth and his addressees. That is, he had to find a relevant place to apply the gospel to them. One size does not fit all in evangelism, so Paul found a point of contact in his hearers through their religiosity. But then the question is, how does one find this point of contact? In brief, the point of contact between the gospel and the hearer is the point at which the person is suppressing God's truth most energetically.[16] We know from what Paul says elsewhere that every human being knows from creation and from implanted testimony that there is a God who should be sought (Rom. 1:18–20; 2:15). Paul is insistent that God has revealed enough of himself to every human being that each one should "seek" (lit. "grope") after him (Acts 17:27)—they are without excuse (Rom. 1:20–21). He began with the Athenians' religion because it was the point at which they were suppressing most energetically the knowledge that God had revealed to them about himself. From creation they knew his eternal power and divine nature. Their own poets had given them a vocabulary by which their suppression would come to the surface—they admitted that God had created them (Acts 17:28). The hundreds of idols surrounding them were an indictment of their attempts to drown out the screaming testimony that there is one God who calls his image bearers to seek him. The most condemning evidence was their idol containing the inscription, "to an unknown god" (Acts 17:23). They had suppressed the truth about God received from creation, and that became the point of contact for the truth of the gospel. A point of contact may be a person's convictions regarding family, his interpretation of suffering, her denial of the person of Christ, his challenge to the reliability of the Scriptures, her hopelessness in a crisis, or his unwillingness to give up control of some cherished sin. And that point of suppression is the point of contact for the gospel.

After Paul established the point of suppression, he submitted evidence that demonstrated that his listeners knew the truth they were suppressing. They knew that the world was created (Acts 17:24), that God is self-sufficient (v. 25), that all people come from one man (v. 26), and that God is the ordainer and sustainer of history (vv. 26, 28). He shot them with their own intellectual bullets. For instance, a deconstructionist author who argues that words cannot convey meaning must be shown that she is relating her ideas in books and lectures. The religion teacher who insists that all roads lead to heaven must admit to practicing the law of noncontradiction. And the postmodern architect who designs staircases that go nowhere and doorways that run into brick walls must reveal in his design plans that the whole structure rests on a predictably designed foundation. There is always evidence that one really believes the truth one is denying. Somewhere the light one is trying to conceal will slip through one's fingers.

After exposing their point of suppression, Paul called his listeners to repentance. While there is no note of sarcasm or disrespect and every evidence of gentleness, Paul nevertheless firmly and authoritatively called his new friends to repentance. He did not commend them for getting close to the truth and then leave them in their darkness. Neither did he applaud them for how far up the ladder to God they had climbed. Instead he exposed that they had fallen all the way down it and that they were trying to climb a ladder made of water, as Van Til the apologist used to say.[17]

Paul provided four timeless inducements to repentance. The first is God's patience (v. 30). Paul said elsewhere that God's kindness leads to repentance (Rom. 2:4). In other words, recognition that God has kindly restrained his judgment thus far should induce the sinner to return. Second, God commands repentance (Acts 17:30). The same God whom everyone must admit created and controls the universe demands that his creatures turn to him alone for salvation. Third, Paul warned that if one does not receive salvation in the way God has prescribed, one will suffer judgment at the day of reckoning (v. 31). Finally, Paul backs every doubter into a corner with his last undeniable piece of evidence—the resurrection of Jesus Christ from the dead. Paul was tried in every major Jewish and Roman court for his belief in the resurrection, and not one could prove the resurrection false. The resurrection of Christ is the checkmate to all contests to Christianity and is a call to lay down one's arms lest one die an eternal death.

The Christian faith can withstand whatever question or attack is brought against it because the truth of the gospel empowered by the Spirit is able to penetrate, convert, and renew the will of any unbeliever. Out of love, the evangelist must not back down from any challenge. Listen carefully and lovingly to questions. Pray for insight into what is provoking the questions. Gently probe to find the points of suppression and expose the inconsistencies. And then compassionately but firmly surround the friend with the evidence of the resurrection and call him or her to repentance that leads to life.

CONCLUSION

Evangelism is God's work of growing his family to an inestimable number who will be gathered before him at the great day (Rev. 7:9). It should be no surprise, therefore, that the same God who "created all things, so that through the church the manifold wisdom of God might now be made known" (Eph. 3:9–10) would ordain manifold ways through which to *proclaim* the gospel. What dignity the Father affords to his children to include them in the causality of bringing the lost to salvation! In response to the inestimable love of God in Christ (2 Cor. 5:14), the evangelist must *persuade* through testimony, invitation, intentional conversation, compassion, and intellectual answers. And out of confidence in the sovereign grace of God, the tearful witness must *pray* that the Spirit would bring in his harvest of souls redounding to the praise of God's glorious grace (Ps. 126:6; Matt. 9:38; Eph. 1:6).

NOTES

1 Michael Duduit, *Handbook of Contemporary Preaching* (Nashville: Broadman, 1992), 525.

2 D. J. Bosch, "Mission and Evangelism: Clarifying the Concepts," *ZM* 68, no. 3 (July 1984): 161–91.

3 Emilio Castro and Gerhard Linn, "Evangelism," in *The Encyclopedia of Christianity*, vol. 2, eds. E. Fahlbusch et al. (Grand Rapids: Eerdmans, 2001), 219.

4 E. Fahlbusch et al., eds., *The Encyclopedia of Christianity*, vol. 3 (Grand Rapids: Eerdmans, 2003), 205.

5 "The Lausanne Covenant," *The Lausanne Movement*, accessed May 15, 2013, http://www.lausanne.org/en/documents/lausanne-covenant.html.

6 See Eugene Peterson's effective summary of Israel's trials throughout Old Testament history in *A Long Obedience in the Same Direction* (Downers Grove: Intervarsity Press, 1980), 94–98.

7 John Wesley, *A Christian Library: Extracts from and Abridgements of the Choicest Pieces of Practical Divinity Which Have Been Published in the English Tongue* (London: T. Cordeux, 1819), 359.

8 Leon Morris, quoted in R. Kent Hughes, *Luke*, vol. 2 (Wheaton: Crossway, 1998), 116.

9 William Barclay, *The Gospel of Luke* (Philadelphia: Westminster Press, 1975), 192.

10 Barna Research Group, "Evangelism Is Most Effective among Kids," (October 11, 2004), www.barna.org. Used by permission.

11 Thom Rhainer, *Effective Evangelistic Churches* (Nashville: Broadman and Holman, 1996).

12 C. H. Spurgeon, *Autobiography: Volume 2: The Full Harvest 1860–1892* (Edinburgh: Banner of Truth, 1976), 241–45.

13 Ibid., 246–48.

14 Insights into these two verses comes from Sinclair Ferguson, *The Sermon on the Mount* (Edinburgh: Banner of Truth, 2009), 55–66.

15 Glenn C. Loury, *One by One from the Inside Out* (New York: The Free Press, 1995), 313.

16 This terminology comes from Henry Krabbendam, "Evangelism and Apologetics" (unpublished syllabus, Covenant College, 1987).

17 Cornelius Van Til, *The Defense of the Faith* (Philadelphia: Presbyterian & Reformed, 1972), 102.